WHO I AM

Tha Ono

ISBN:
Hardbound-978-621-470-629-7
Softbound/Paperback-978-621-470-630-3
MOBI/KINDLE-978-621-470-631-0

Published by:
Poetry Planet Book Publishing House
Rosario, Pozorrubio, Pangasinan, Philippines
Contact Number: 09554960094
Email: maritesritumalta@gmail.com

TABLE OF CONTENTS

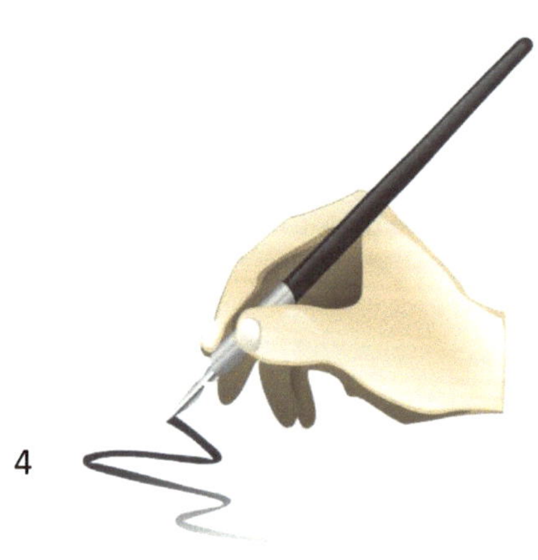

Dear Reader

I am a poem, built upon words that flow like a river. My words hold secrets and stories, written in a language that only the heart can understand. I am a mixture of emotion, a journey through the human experience, a reflection of life.

My words in this phase though self-centred are the keys that unlock the doors of hidden meanings. Each line, a snapshot of an emotion, a thought, or a moment captured in time. My words are the brushstrokes of a masterpiece, each one significant in its own way, each one adding to the beauty of the whole.

I am a poem, the sum of my parts. I am the rhythm that pulses through your veins, the cadence that sets your heart alight. I am the voice of the soul, the language of the heart, and the beat of the mind.

My words are the messengers, sent to carry the weight of emotions too heavy to bear, too difficult to express. They are a balm that heals wounds, a light that illuminates the darkness, and a spark that sets the soul ablaze.

I am a poem, and my words are my magic. They transport you to worlds beyond your imagination, to places where dreams come to life, where the impossible becomes possible. And even as they flow from my pen, they continue to evolve, to grow, to change. For I am a poem, and I am eternal.

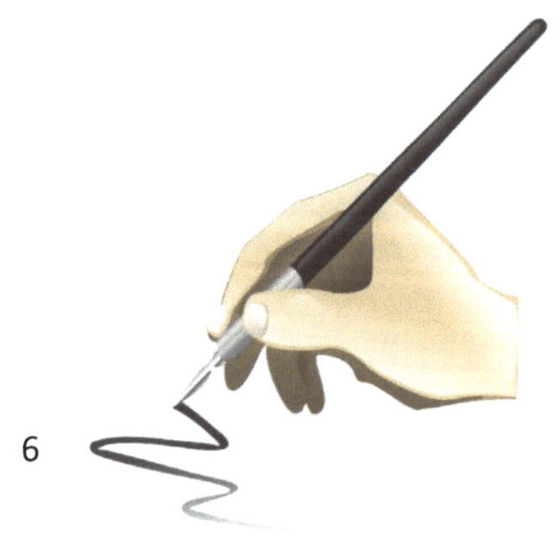

MY MIND AND ME

My mind and me, we often roam...
Through the vast expanse of thought...
Exploring all the depths unknown...
All the wonders we have looked for...

We journey through the winding paths...
Memories both old and new...
Contemplating life's aftermaths...
All the things we wish to do...

We ponder on the mysteries...
Love, of pain, of joy, of strife...
All the hidden histories...
That shape the fabric of our life...

Mind and me, we often dream...
Things we hope to be...
Places we have seen...
In visions of our reverie...

We imagine worlds beyond our own...
Delve into the unknown realms...
Dancing among the stars alone...
In fanciful, ethereal helms...

We conjure up fantastic tales...
Heroes, villains, quests, and wars...
Allowing our imaginations sail...
To distant lands and distant shores...

Mind and me, we sometimes clash...
When worries, doubts, and fears arise...
Thoughts become a tangled mesh...
As stress and anxiety disguise...

We find a way to heal...
Work through all the turmoil's din...
Later rather than sooner we are back to what we
feel...
In harmony once more within...

My mind and me, we are never still...
As thoughts and ideas ebb and flow...
Though we may not always thrill...
We keep on moving, as we know...

That life's a journey, full of change...
We must keep on growing too...
Though the path may sometimes range...
We shall face it all, me, and my mind, true...

STILL ALIVE

In times of strife and trouble...
When chaos reigns supreme...
It is easy to feel lost and broken...
Like a cracked and shattered dream...

Even in the darkest hour...
When hope seems far away...
There is a spark that still burns bright...
Refusing to fade away...

It's the fire that keeps us going...
The flame that guides us through...
A light that shines inside of us...
A love that is pure and true...

When we are knocked down...
Our strength may start to wane...
We rise again, unbroken...
Stronger than before, with the will to sustain...

Hold on tight to that ember...
That still burns deep inside...
Though the road may be long and hard...
You are still alive, still thriving, still fighting the good
fight...

ANYONE

No one hears me when I speak...
Words just fade into the week...
My voice falls silent to the ground...
As the noise around me keeps its loud sound...

Picked for all the dirty work...
Underestimated, I remain as a clerk...
Giving and giving, until I am all used up...
Bound by my duties, feeling like a pup...

Value is measured by what I can do...
None pays attention to the glue...
That holds everything together, unappreciated...
Belittled, fooled, unloved, and understated...

Dream of a world where my voice heard...
A place where worth is not only word...
A place where deeds and voice align...
True greatness is rightly assigned...

I grow tired of being passed over...
Always seen as the doer...
Want my voice to soar like a bird...
Valued for who I am, not what I owned...

I found peace in a quiet zone...
I found an inner strength to call my own...
To stand tall and believe I can...
Not allowing anyone underestimate my plan...

Will not let others' opinions define...
Nor can I let their actions undermine...
That deep within my heart, I know...
That I am worth more than they will ever show...

Take back control of my life...
Stand firm and refuse to strive...
To make everyone else happy while crying a tear...
For they shall never listen to me, but I can clearly
hear...

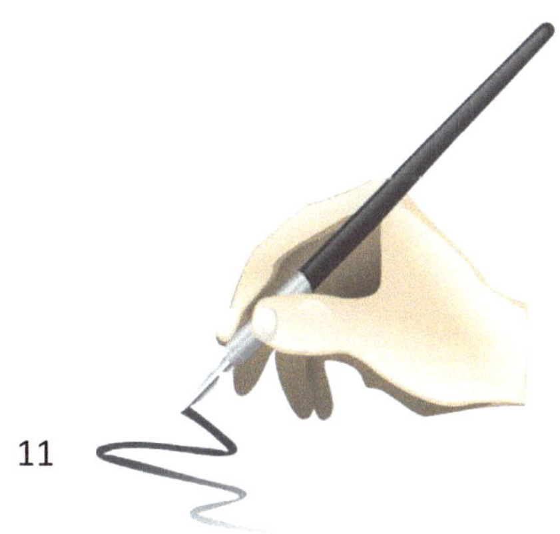

JEALOUS

Jealousy wells up inside my heart...
As I see others reach the top of the chart...
Wondering why that cannot be me...
Blind to all the good that I can see...

Look in the mirror and see flaws...
Ignoring the beauty that I should applaud...
Believing that I am not good enough...
That my efforts will always be tough...

I envy the ones who seem to have it all...
Their success and happiness make me feel small...
I wish I could be like them...
I'm lost in jealousy's pit and forget to stem...

The fear of failure and not reaching the mark...
Drives me to compare and despair, leaving a dark...
Hole in my heart that I try to fill...
With the hope that one day, I'll also thrill...

Joy cannot come from misplaced envy...
Nor satisfaction from things that do not belong to
me...
Must find my own path and shine...

Embrace my unique talents and not cross over the
line...

Must learn to appreciate my worth...
Understand that my value stretches beyond earth...
In the end, it is not about what others achieve...
What I can do cause it's mine to receive...

I lay aside my jealousy and fear...
Choosing to value myself, to be clear...
Rejoicing in the things I must give...
Learning to love myself, to live...

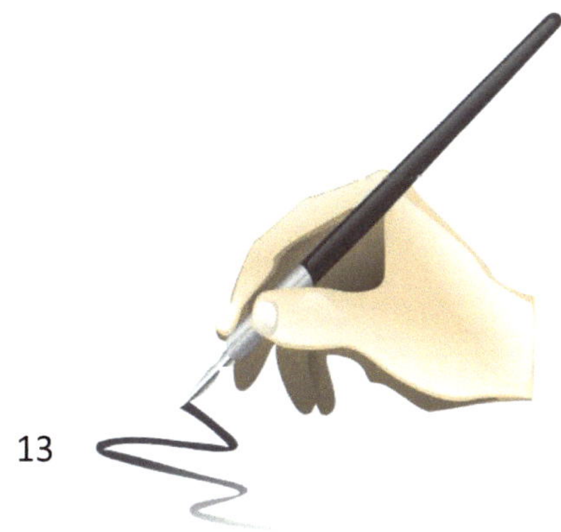

MASTERMIND

Mastermind, a creator of worlds...
A dream weaver, with limitless swirls...
My imagination, a canvas so broad...
I paint with thoughts, transcending the flawed...

I weave tales of love, of heartbreak and pain...
Crafting a mosaic, in words to sustain...
Each stroke, a piece of my soul on display...
A reflection of me, in every which way...

I am a mastermind, of life's grand design...
A weaver of tales, both yours and mine...
Through my prose, I unveil the mystery...
Emotions, up close and history...

Spin a song that speaks to your heart...
A feeling that tears your world apart...
Flicker of emotion, you will see...
Your truth, your pain, and your destiny....
Mastermind, a creator of worlds...
A sculptor of stories, that forever swirls...
My words, a prism, of love's pure light...
A tapestry woven, with passion and insight...

Take my hand, and dive deep within...

Let me take you to places, you have never been...
Within my words, you will find the key...
To unlock the doors of your heart, so free...

I am a mastermind, of life's grand design...
A storyteller, of love's sweet sign...
Embark with me, on a journey so grand...
Within my words, we shall find love's full hand...

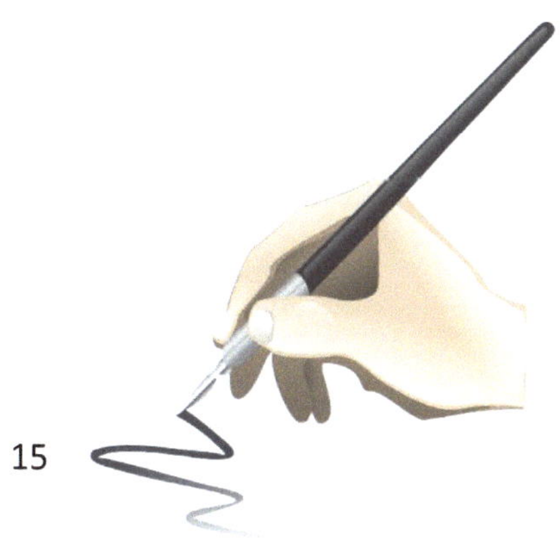

WORDS I NEVER SAID

Sometimes the words I never said...
The ones that linger in my head...
They collect like storm clouds on the vista...
Whispers of pain, love, and life's endless distance...

Pain, an expert in disguise...
I can hide it well behind my eyes...
Ache in my heart never truly leaves...
It is a constant reminder of all that grieves...

Love, a complicated dance...
A union of emotional happenstance...
It can bring me to my knees, a heart aflame...
Before throwing me, like a moth to a flame...

Words I never said, about love and its power...
Moments that fly by, in love's fickle hour...
It can break me down or lift me high...
A rollercoaster ride that never seems to die...

Life is a journey, twisted and bright...
A twenty-six-mile journey of dark and light...
Words I never said, the thoughts that linger...
Moments that pass, with a flicker...

Memories that haunt me, of love and loss...
It is the price I pay for love's sweet gloss...
Highs and lows of life, it is the never-ending
journey...
A dance with fate, a balancing act in which we learn
to earn...

Despite the pain, the joys, the strife...
I keep moving forward, grasping life...
In the end, it's the moments we have shared...
Words I never said, the love that we dared...

People I have met, the memories we have made...
Lessons learned; the paths laid...
It is the words I never said, that echo on...
In the corners of my heart, the love that has gone...

In the end, it is the journey that counts...
Steps taken, the moments that mount...
Life is fleeting, and love is pure...
In the end, it is the love that endures...

I'll take the words I never said...
Let them be the lessons that mark my head...
In pain, love, and life, we find our way...
Through the storm clouds, to brighter days...

BAD BLOOD

Dear Bad Blood, I have got something to say...
We have been friends for a while, in our own unique
way...
Lately, things just do not seem right...
It's like we are drifting apart, like day and night...

We have been there for you through thick and thin...
Lately, the drama's too much to take in...
I am tired of the negativity and strife...
It's time to move on, and start a new life...

Always cherish the memories we share...
It is time to let go, and show that I care...
It is not easy to say goodbye to a friend...
Sometimes, it is for the best, in the end...

Here's to you, Bad Blood, may you find your way...
I will always remember you, day by day...
Moving on, to new horizons and more...
Wishing you all the best, from my core...
Though we shall never walk together again upon
life's shore...

DELICATE

I am a man with a delicate heart...
One that beats with love right from the start...
My emotions run deep; my feelings are true...
Vulnerability is something I pursue...

Heart is not steel...
That does not mean I cannot feel...
I am not afraid to let tears flow...
To show affection and let love to grow...

I am a man who's not afraid to say...
"I love you" in my own special way...
I will write you poems and songs...
Tell you love stories all night long...

My heart is open, it is plain to see...
Love is what sets me free...
May not fit the mould of what you have seen...
My delicate heart is what makes me keen...
Do not judge me by my fragile parts...
I am a man with a delicate heart...
My love is strong, it will never depart...
I will always wear it on my sleeve, from the start...

MEANT TO LIVE

I am meant to live...
Breathe in the world...
Embrace with an open heart...
Wear my soul unfurled...

Meant to feel...
Let my spirit flourish...
Dance with wild abandon...
Allow my energy to nourish...

Meant to realise...
Gaze upon the wonder...
Explore this vast universe...
Absorb, grow, and ponder...

Meant to love, cherish and to care...
Bringing light to dark corners...
Spread kindness everywhere...

Meant to live...
Fulfilling every moment...
Chase my passions fiercely...
To be awe-inspiring and potent...

Will embrace life...

All that it entails...
Will let my spirit shine...
Telling my incredible tales...

I am meant to live...
Live well and true...
Will leave my mark...
By being gloriously, authentically, and beautifully
you...

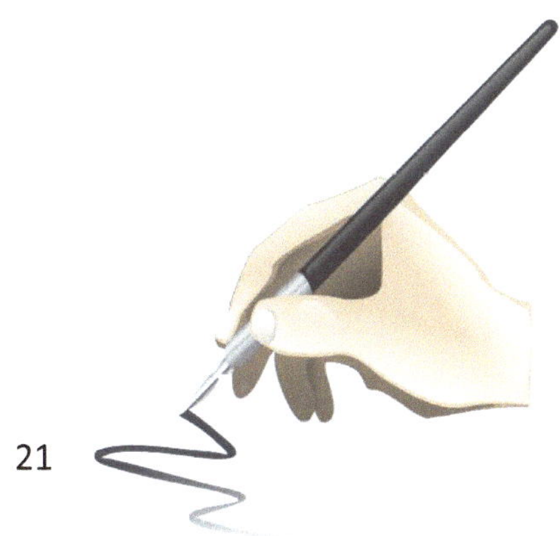

WHITE HORSE

Life, my white horse, galloping free...
On the vast expanse of a limitless sea...
A journey of adventure, a ride of a lifetime...
Untethered, unbridled, unafraid of the climb...

My white horse, a symbol of my will to live...
Untamed, bold, and ready to give...
Strength, courage, and unyielding faith...
Conquer and overcome whatever fate...

Through life's trials and hardships, I go...
My white horse, my companion, never to slow....
Pushing forward, towards the horizon...
Chasing dreams, without compromise or treason...

Though sometimes storms may come and rage...
My white horse endures, never to disengage...
Undefeated, unbeaten, an unwavering force...
Life, my white horse, on a never-ending course...

I ride, with my head held high...
My white horse beneath me, flying by...
Conquering my fears, to conquer the strife...
To live my life on a white horse of life...

REPUTATION

My reputation, like a shadow that follows me...
Preceding me into every room I enter...
Held words behind my back...
Murmurs that hint of hidden agendas....

A reputation, both a curse and a blessing...
Born of the words and actions of yesterday...
Solidified by the eyes that are watching...
Marking everything I do, and what I say...

Reputation is my best friend...
The foundation of my credibility...
I feel it more like burdens that never end...
A weighty shroud of invisibility...

Walking on a tightrope, every day...
Afraid to make a single misstep that may...
Add fuel to the fire that never seems to abate...
My reputation a harsh judge and jury, never to
abdicate...

Still, I am me, regardless of what they say...
Reputation, just echoes of yesterday...
A static reminder of the story's others tells...
But they are not me, and they cannot tell me how to dwell...

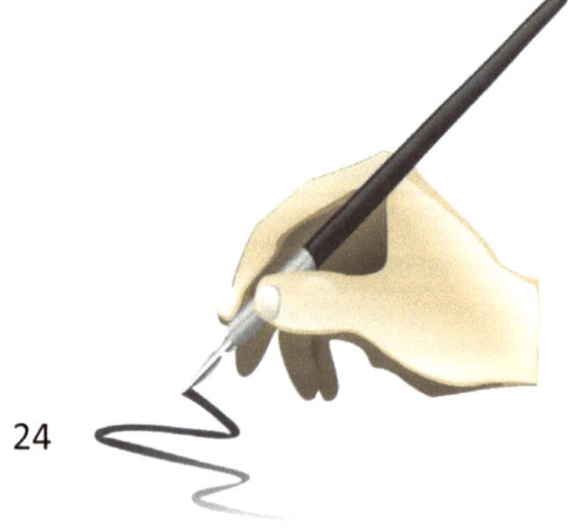

JADED

Jaded, worn out, and tired of it all...
Heart beats slow, my spirit falls...
Life's colours have faded, and all that's left...
Shades of grey, a world bereft...

Once I was young and full of dreams...
Now it seems, they are bursting at the seams...
Reality's harsh, and it has taken its toll...
Leaving me jaded, empty, and cold...

I long for something to reignite my fire...
Lift me up, take me higher...
Weight of the world keeps me down...
Dragging me deeper, until I drown...

Is there a way to break free from this lavender
haze???
Seeing the world through fresh eyes, and blaze...
A trail that is new, and full of wonder...
Shaking off this jadedness, and not go under???

Release the past as the present lay...
Embrace the unknown with open arms, at last...
Find the beauty in the simple things...

See the world as if for the first time, and spread my
wings...

Though I may be jaded now...
Know deep down, there is still a spark somehow...
A glimmer of hope, a ray of light...
That will guide me through the darkest night...

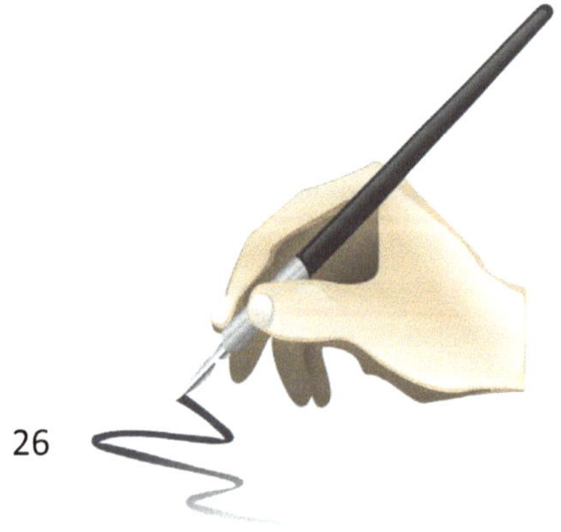

ANTI-HERO

I am the Anti Hero, the one who walks alone...
The one who stands against the tide, the one who's
never known...
I'm not your shining knight in black armour, I'm not
your perfect saint...
I'm the one who's flawed and broken, the one who
bears the taint...

My heart is dark and troubled, my soul is filled with
doubt...
I've made mistakes and bad decisions; I've taken the
wrong route...
I've hurt the ones I loved the most, I've caused them
pain and strife...
I've lived my life without a cause, without a purpose
or a drive...

Still, I stand, with head held high, with courage in my
heart...
I'll fight against the darkness; I'll play my own part...
I'll be the one who takes a stand, who fights for what
is right...
Even if it means I'll fall, even if it means I'll fight alone
at night...

I'm the Anti Hero, the one who walks the line...
Between the darkness and the light, between the
pain and the divine...
I will be the one who stands his ground, who fights
against the odds...
I'll be the one who breaks the chains, who rises and
nods...

If you see me walking by, don't judge me by my
past...
Don't see me as a villain, a rebel, or an outcast...
I am the Anti Hero, the one who'll never yield...
The one who'll fight until the end, the one who'll
never yield...

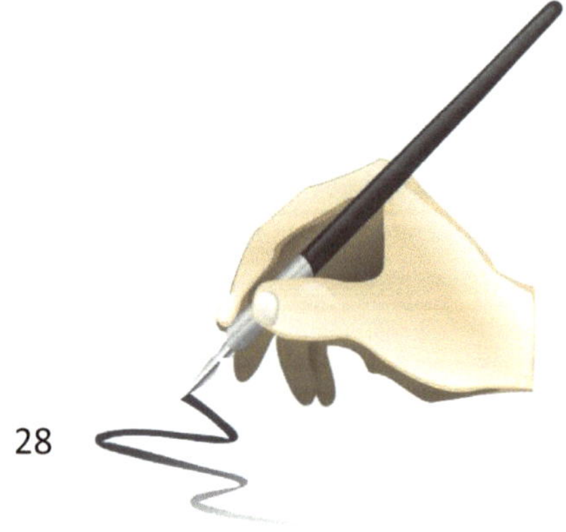

BACK TO BLACK

In the depths of darkness, I'll find my way...
Back to a time when everything was grey...
My heart was heavy, my soul was black...
I couldn't see the light, couldn't find my track...

Now know, I can turn around...
Can leave the shadows and the underground...
Face my fears, I will break the chains...
I'll find the light, and break the stains...

I'll go back to black, but not in sorrow...
I'll find the strength to face tomorrow...
I'll wear my scars with pride and grace...
I'll find my way back to my rightful place...

In the darkness, I'll find my light...
In the blackness, I'll find my strength to fight...
I'll rise above, I'll shine so bright...
From the shadows, I'll take my flight...

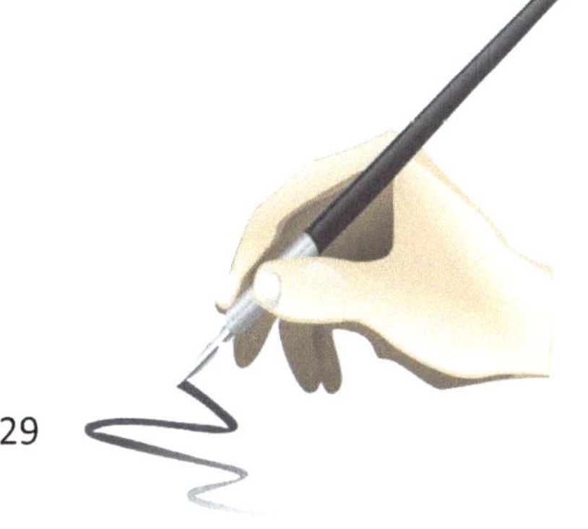

ME, MYSELF, AND I

We walk this path alone...
Through the twists and turns of life, we have grown...
Together we stand, a trio of one...
Facing the world, until our days done...

Me, the one who feels and breathes...
With a heart that aches and a soul that grieves...
I am the one who loves and laughs...
Who cries and hurts, who walks life's paths...

Myself, the one who thinks and plans...
With a mind that wanders and a heart that
understands...
I am the one who dreams and schemes...
Who sets goals and reaches for big things...

I, the one who looks and sees...
With eyes that observe and a mind that believes...
I am the one who seeks and finds...
Who explores the world and expands my mind...

Together we make a formidable team...
With strengths and weaknesses, seen...
In the end, it is just us three...
Me, myself, and I, forever free...

May we walk with heads held high...
With courage and grace, and never a sigh...
We are one, and one we will be...
Me, myself, and I, eternally...

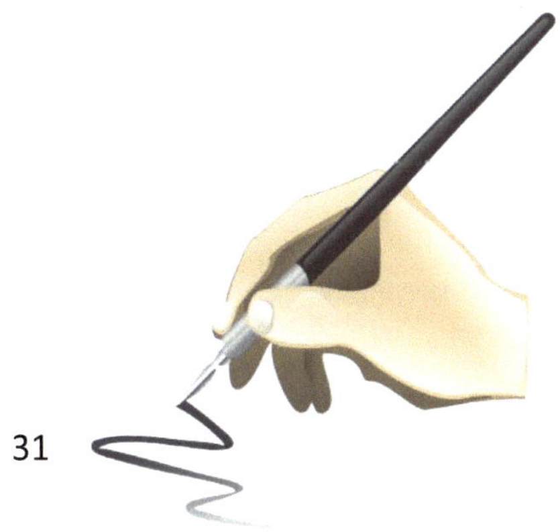

EMOTIONS

A tempestuous sea...
Raging and roaring, consuming me...
A maelstrom of feelings, a hurricane of pain...
A never-ending storm inside my brain...

Sadness and grief, they weigh me down...
Sorrow and heartache, they wear me out...
Loneliness and despair, they haunt my soul...
Anguish and torment, they take their toll...

Try to fight, to keep my head above...
Find some peace, some light, some love...
Waves keep crashing, the winds keep howling...
My heart keeps breaking, my spirit bowing...

I wish for calm, for quiet, for rest...
Respite from the turmoil, a moment of blessedness...
Storm rages on, with no end in sight...
I'm lost in the darkness, with no hope in sight...

Holding on, to a glimmer of hope...
A ray of light, a way to cope...
Even amid the storm...
There's a chance for healing, a chance to transform...

I ride the waves, and weather the gale...
My tragic emotions, my heart on sale...
Though the storm may never truly end...
I will find a way to survive, to heal, to mend...

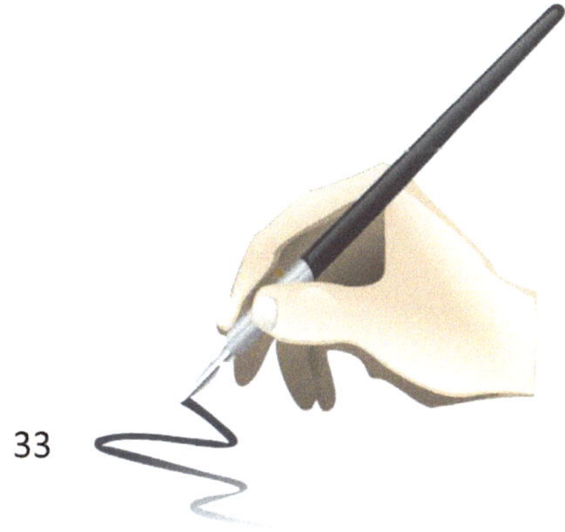

LAST RESORT

My mind is a labyrinth, I am lost and confused...
My heart is heavy, my soul is bruised...
I've searched for answers, I've prayed for strength...
Nothing seems to make sense; nothing seems to
lengthen...

My last resort, my final hope...
Is the pen and paper, my only scope...
Pour my heart out, I bare my soul...
I write my pain away, I try to be whole...

In this world of chaos, this sea of tears...
My words are my anchor, my shield from fears...
I write of love, of hope and light...
I create my own world, where everything's right...

In this world I find my peace...
Where my worries and doubts finally cease...
I find my solace, my sanctuary...
In the words I write, my sanctuary...

When life gets tough, when everything is dark...
It seems like my world's falling apart...
Turn to my pen, my faithful friend...
And write my way through, until the end...

ALL TOO WELL

All too well, I remember the pain...
Hurt that lingered, like an unwelcome stain...
It seeped through my bones, and ate at my soul...
Leaving me broken, feeling out of control...

All too well, I recall the tears that fell...
Hours of awful, that seemed to swell...
The emptiness that echoed, all around...
Tried to find the strength to stand my ground...

All too well, I can still feel the ache...
Heart shattered, just like a break...
Moments passed, when I felt so alone...
Fearing that nothing would ever atone...

All too well, I know the scars it left...
Memories that haunt, like a lonely grand theft...
Sleepless nights, which felt like endless days...
Pain that lingers, in so many ways...

All too well, I've learned to find my way...
I leal my wounds, and chase the pain away...
Hold onto hope, and find love once more...
Let the memories fade, like waves upon the shore...

REVIVAL

With every breath that I take...
I feel my revival, my inner strength awakes...
I am rising from the ashes, like a phoenix reborn...
Leaving behind my worries, fears and forlorn...

My revival is my journey to my inner light...
A path that leads me to my own insight...
I am chasing my dreams and following my heart...
Breaking free from the chains that had fallen apart...

Revival is my fight against despair...
Shedding the weight of the burdens I can no longer
bear...
I am determined to rise above my pain...
Tear down my walls and break the chains...

Revival is my journey of self-love...
Embracing every inch of me, as I soar above...
I am taking every step with renewed grace...
Living life to the fullest, with a smile on my face...

So let me rise higher, and let me be free...
Let me be who I am, unapologetically...
Revival is my journey of growth and self-discovery...

A journey of resilience, and strength untold and discovered...

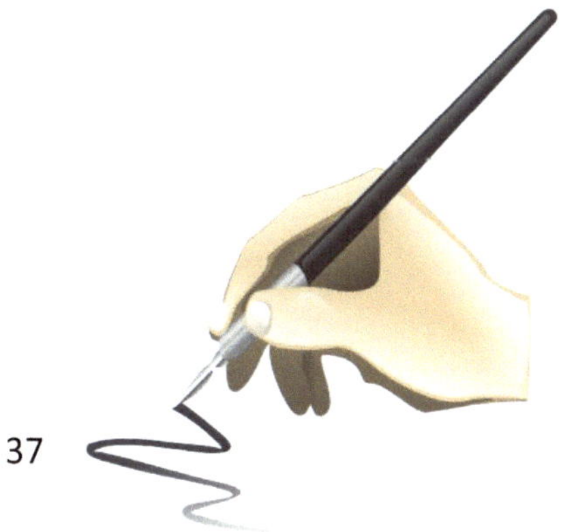

SOME KIND OF NARCISSIST

The Narcissist within, oh how it thrives...
It seeks attention and validation for its lives...
A grandiose sense of self, an ego unmatched...
It believes it's a star, a diamond unmatched...

Narcissist within, it craves admiration...
It needs constant praise and celebration...
It is a prima donna, a diva in its ways...
It is a king, a queen, a ruler to laud always...

Narcissist within, it lacks empathy...
It barely cares for others' misery...
It is all about them, it's all about their world...
Others' feelings do not matter, they are just a silly
twirl...

This Narcissist within, oh it is hard to tame...
It is almost impossible to put it to shame...
It thinks it's perfect, it thinks it's divine...
Its sense of entitlement is constant, it's hard to
decline...

Deep inside, this Narcissist within...
Is just a scared child, expressing its sin...
It is a mirror, reflecting years of hurt and pain...
It is a cry for love, a yearning to be humane...

Let us not judge the Narcissist within...
With love and compassion, we can surely begin...
Help him heal, to help them find his way...
Love himself and others every day...

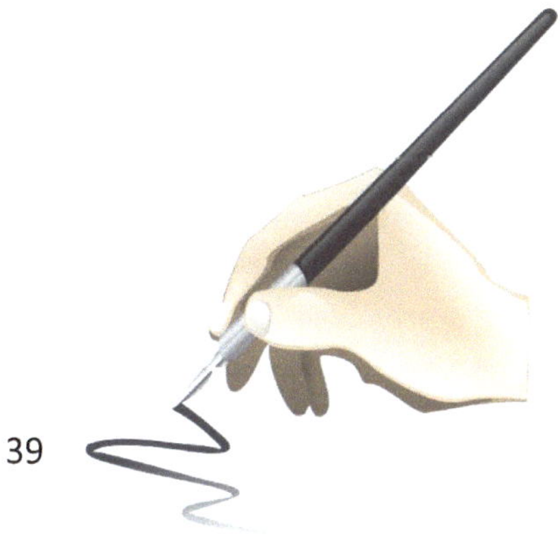

UNHOLY

My unholy mind is a chaotic place...
A world of darkness and a lost race...
Thoughts shrouded in shadows and fears...
Soul is stained from fallen tears...

See demons lurking in every corner...
Whispers of hell and wicked orders...
Mind plays tricks on me every day...
Tempting me to sin and lead me astray...

Deep down that the light still shines...
Awaiting my salvation, my heart to align...
I must fight the darkness with all my might...
Embrace the love that offers me sight...

Though my unholy mind may be a curse...
It can also be a blessing, a poetic verse...
In my pain and brokenness, I find...
Beauty in life, the purpose to unwind...

Can say with certainty and grace...
My unholy mind will find its rightful place...
In the arms of the one who died for me...
To set me free and heal my misery...

KARMA

Karma is a friend of mine, a true companion...
It follows me wherever I go...
Reminds me of every little action...
Seeds that I sow...

It whispers to me in the quiet moments...
In the instants when I am alone...
Telling me to be mindful...
Seeds I have sewn...

Every kindness shown to others...
Every gesture of love and care...
Returned to me in abundance...
A gift beyond compares...

Every misstep, every mistake...
An unkind word or selfish deed...
Comes the bitter harvest, the toll I must pay...
Until I learn to plant the right seed...
Karma is a reminder...
Have power that lies within...
Shaping my life and destiny...
Deeds that I begin...

Choose my actions wisely...
With compassion, love, and grace...
Karma will guide me...
To a brighter, more beautiful place...

42

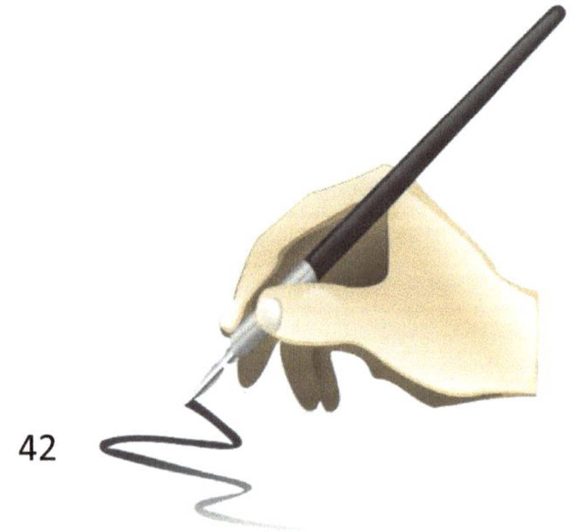

RISE

Rise from the ashes...
Of what once was...
Spirit unbroken...
Will unyielding...

Revolt against...
Shackles of doubt...
Chains of fear...
Against the weight of despair...

Rise to face...
Challenges ahead...
To conquer my fears...
To overcome my doubts...

Rise with strength...
With courage and grace...
With a fire in my heart...
Light on my face...

Rise to be...
The person I was meant to be...
To live my life fully...
Be free...
No more chain linked fences around me...

Let me rise...
Let me shine...
Let me be the person, that I know I can be...

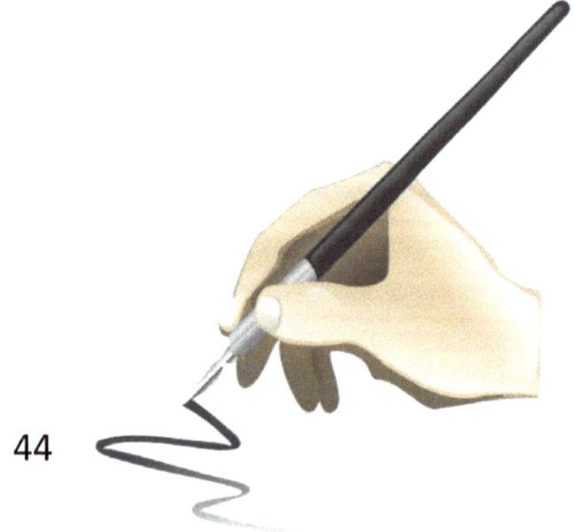

BORN TO DIE

Born to die...
To leave this world behind...
To say goodbye to all I have known...
Leave no trail behind...

My life is but a journey...
A path I must traverse...
Though the end is certain...
The route is mine to choose...

Travel through this world...
Take in all its sights...
Though my time is brief...
Like a river as it flows...

Every moment counts...
Every breath is precious...
Though we cannot change our fate...
Our memories will guide us...

Live your life with purpose...
Make every moment count...
In the end, it is not the length of life...
You will realize it has always been the quality that
truly counts...

READY FOR IT

Ready for love, it was real...
A feeling that I could not conceal...
My heart was open, my soul felt free...
When will you come, to completed me???

The way you will smile, the twinkle in your eyes...
I can hear you laugh, that makes my heart rise...
With every touch, my heart would skip...
A love I never thought I'd find in a glimpse...

You shall show me a love that's pure...
A love that's real, simple, and sure...
You will take my hand, and show me the way...
In your arms, I know my fears would sway...

Together we will create memories to last...
A love that's pure, too precious to be passed...
Though our paths have taken us apart...
Our love will one day meet in fate, deep in my
heart...

Ready for love, if it is real...
Though we have never met, I know we will...
The love we will share, will be true...
A love that will stay, forever anew....

I WRITE SINS NOT TRAGEDIES

I write sins not tragedies, with pen and paper in
hand...
Staring at the blank page, trying to understand...
What is it that I want to say, what is it that I feel...
What is it that I want to scream, what is it that I
conceal...

Write sins not tragedies, the words they flow like
fire...
A cathartic release, a burning desire...
To let it all out, to make sense of the mess...
To give a voice to the things I struggle to express...

Write sins not tragedies, my heart it beats out loud...
As I pour my soul out onto the page, without a single
doubt...
That these words, these sins, these tragedies, and
all...
Reflect the highs and lows of my rise and my fall...

I write sins not tragedies, not to wallow in despair...
Allowing hope to be found amid the pain that I
bare...
To find meaning in the chaos, and beauty in the
storm...

Knowing that I am not alone, if I write in this form...

So let me write my sins, let me write my tragedies...
Let me pour out my heart, let me set it free...
Every word, every line, every verse that I create...
Is a part of who I am, and has led me to this place...

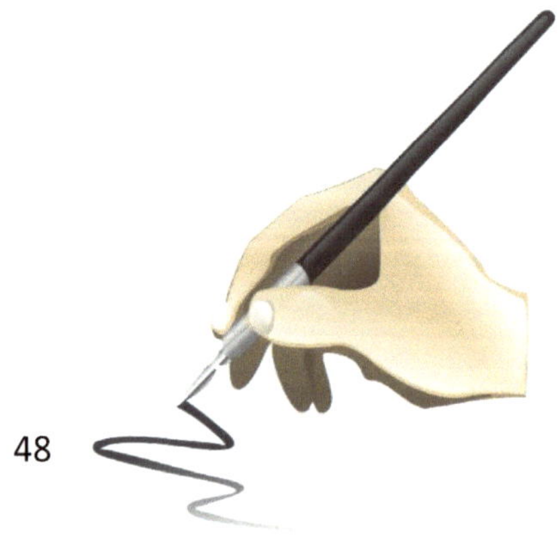

48

THE GREATEST

Seed, a small and humble soul...
Yet I dream of greatness, of a towering goal...
Wonder what the future holds, what I will become...
With hard work and effort, I will surely overcome...

I will be a great man, strong and confident...
With wisdom beyond my years, and ironclad intent...
Stand tall in the face of fear, and never falter...
With a heart borne of passion, I will overcome any
alter...

Will be a leader, inspiring others to follow...
A beacon of hope for those who feel hollow...
Shine brighter than the sun, and radiate strength...
I'll never lose sight of my dreams, no matter the
length...

Show love and kindness, and always be true...
To the person I am, and the goals that I pursue...
When my time comes, and I leave this earth...
I'll know that I made a difference, through my
courage and worth...

I am but a seed, but I'll blossom and grow...
To become a great man, whose story others will know...
I will be a shining example of what is possible...
Will always stand strong, even in times that are hostile...

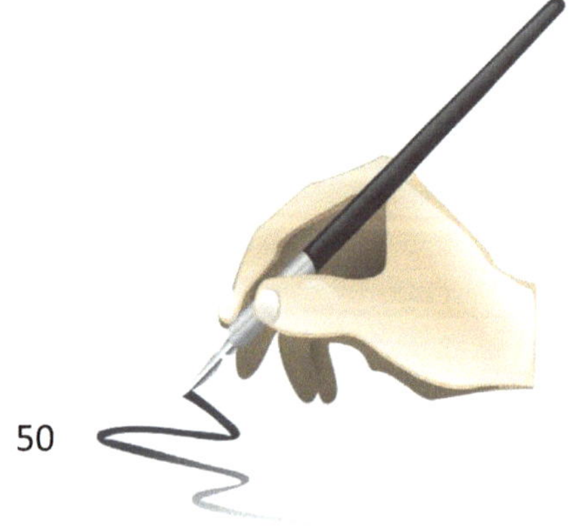

MUSIC

Music in me, music in my life...
It keeps the rhythm beating, it keeps me alive...
When the world is too loud, and my mind is too still...
Music is the magic that sets my soul to thrill...

As a child, I learned I don't have to be perfect to
dance...
To move my feet to the rhythm's chance...
Music flowed through me like a river...
Knew then, I'd always be a lover never a fighter...

Music has been my guide through joy and sorrow...
A beacon of light through the darkest of tomorrow...
It's my source of inspiration when my strength is
low...
A gentle hand to guide me when the path is
unknown...

In the good times, music lifts me high...
With each note and melody, I soar like a butterfly...
When life is tough, and the pain is real...
Music wraps me up in a blanket of solace and
appeal...

The beat of the drums, the strings of the guitar...

The sound of a voice that fills me near and far...
Music is the language that my heart speaks...
It touches my soul, heals me with such sweet relief...

Music is the journey that I've always known...
To the beats and the rhythms, I've always been
shown...
It's taken me places I never thought possible...
From the depths of my soul, it's been so wonderful...

Music in me, music in my life...
It's the essence of who I am, and why I strive...
It's the light in the darkness, the hope in despair...
It's the joy and the laughter, the peace that I bear...

In every moment, music is my companion...
Guiding my steps, moving me to action...
It's the fire that burns within my soul...
A reminder that I am never alone...

I'll keep dancing to the beat of my own drum...
Allow music to take me to where I've never come...
In its rhythm, I find my life...
In its melody, I've learned to thrive...

MIDNIGHT SKY

In the deep, dark hours of midnight...
I sit alone, wrapped in starlight...
The world around me is calm and still...
As the universe whispers its will...

Thoughts and memories swirl in my head...
As I lie in my soft, cosy bed...
Shadows dance across the walls...
As I ponder life's endless calls...

I think of all the paths I have taken...
Roads that lay ahead, yet unshaken...
My dreams like a map that guides me...
Showing me the way that I must see...

I've lived through love, and heartbreak too...
Felt both joy and sadness through and through...
In each moment, I've found a light...
Guiding me through the darkest of night...
The midnight hour brings peace to my mind...
As I allow my soul to unwind...
Close my eyes and let my thoughts fly...
Drifting away to the stars in the sky...

As the sky shifts from dark to light...

Dawn breaks through the endless night...
I feel a sense of renewal within...
Newfound hope to begin...

Though life may be bittersweet and tough...
Know that I am enough...
To face the challenges that come my way...
Seizing upon each brand-new day...

The midnight hour teaches me to be...
Focused, resilient, and strong, you see...
It reminds me that life is but a fleeting blink...
Every moment's a chance to genuinely think...

In the hours of midnight deep...
When the world around me seems to sleep...
Take comfort in the starry light...
As I embrace my life's journey, late at night...

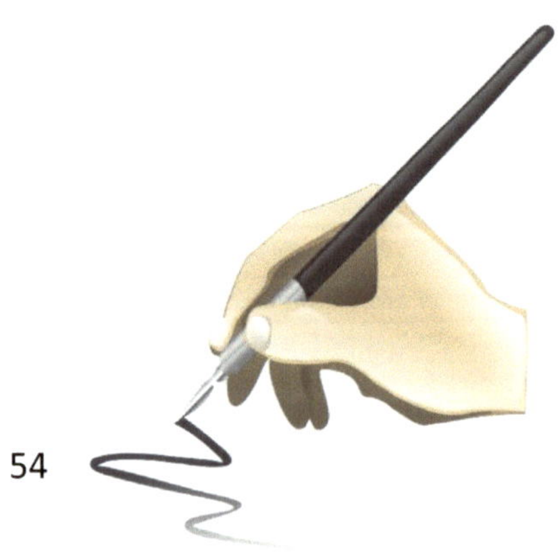

HAVE NOT MET ME YET

Have not met me yet...
Knowing that I am there...
Somewhere deep down inside...
Waiting for its unveiling, to share...

The person that I am...
The one I will come to be...
Each day a step closer...
To the true, authentic me...

Living a life till now...
Still feeing incomplete...
As if there is so much more...
That I've yet to discover and meet...

The passions I will pursue...
The dreams I will finally chase...
All waiting for me to find them...
Finally taking my rightful place...
In a world that seems so endless...
Just a small piece of the whole...
In my own way, I am unique...
Bringing comfort to my soul...

Have not met me yet...

Just know I am on my way...
Each step I take reveals...
A little more of who I will be one day...

Learned that life's a journey...
A chance to find our way...
Along the winding path we will grow...
Into whom we are meant to be someday...

So, I will keep on moving forward...
With an open heart and mind...
Ready for the unknown...
Whatever uncharted territory I may find...

Have not met me yet.
Excited for the day...
When I finally get to meet...
Welcome the real me, no matter what happens...

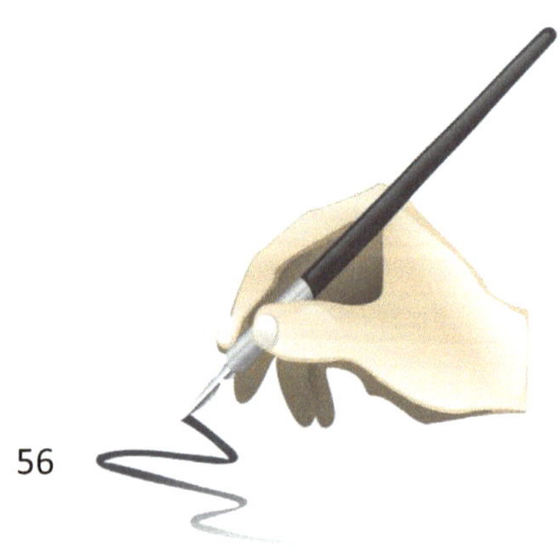

STILL HAVE ME

With every passing day...
I find myself lost in thought...
Thoughts of you that never fade...
Thoughts that keep me caught...

Caught in a trap of longing...
Moments we shared...
Memories that keep coming...
Moments that we both cared...

Cared for each other's presence...
Appreciated for each other's touch...
Wanted for the love we nurtured...
Love that meant so much...

Even though you are gone...

time keeps moving on...
My heart still beats for you...
A love that still lives strong...

Every moment I recall...
The way we used to be...
A time in which love blossomed...
When it was you and me...

Though we are worlds apart...
The memories stay...
Your love still lives within my heart...
I still feel the same...

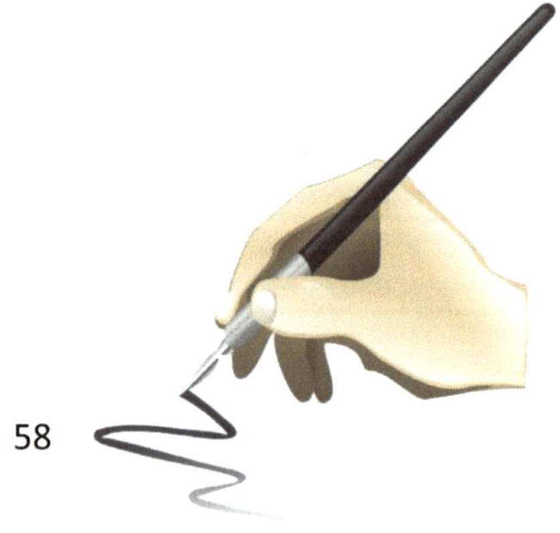

58

WHO I AM...

Advocate for animals and persons with disabilities...
My heart is filled with compassion and immeasurable
abilities...
Saw the power of advocacy and its force...
Seen how it can change lives, of both man and
horse...

Standing up for the ones that cannot speak...
Filled with a passion that is beyond unique...
An overwhelming desire to create change...
Raising awareness, to make a lasting range...

Seen animals treated as less than...
An advocate, I know they deserve more than...
A cruel existence, locked up behind bars...
Exploited for human whims, like cars...

Seen those with disabilities, too...
Mistreated and held back by society's view...
Limited by their inability to hear, see or walk...
Their hearts and minds, not one bit less of a rock...

Advocacy for those who cannot speak...
Reminded of the empathy and the urge we look for...
Making the world a kinder, safer place...

Where every creature treated with fair grace...

We work to build a bridge of understanding and
love...
Hope of a world where opportunity rises above...
Where every animal given a chance to thrive...
Persons with disabilities given their justice...

We focus on changing policy and mindset alike...
Taking small steps every day, one at a time...
To build a world that honours every being...
Showing that we care for and about living things...

Voiceless animals and the persons unable to speak...
We stand up for what is right, and against what we
consider bleak...
We rise above the challenges, and never back
down...
Knowing every being deserves renown...

An advocate, I pledge to keep up the fight...
Working tirelessly in both day and night...
Bringing to light issues to the world...
Creating a better place for every boy and girl...

Join me in this important work...
Let us all make a solemn oath to perk...
Rights of animals and persons with disabilities...
Closer to a world of compassion and more abilities...

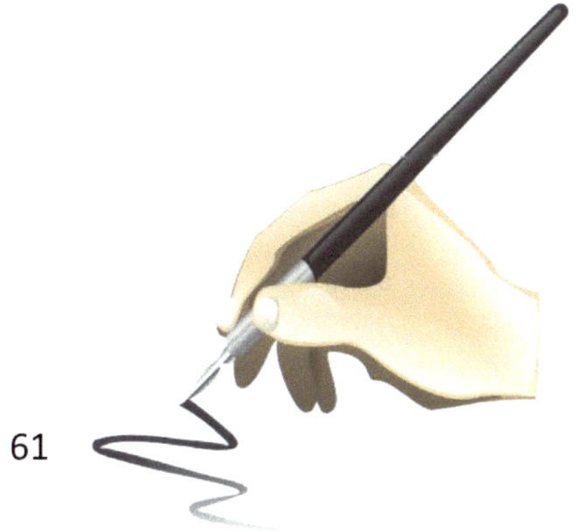

MY NEXT CHAPTER

My next chapter is about to unfold...
A new story waiting to be told...
It is a blank slate, a page yet unwritten...
A future full of potential and completely unbidden...

Leaving behind what no longer serves...
Making space for what I deserve...
It is time for a change, a new direction...
A shift in perspective and a reflection...

Taking a deep breath, and diving in...
Embracing the unknown and all that is within...
The possibilities are endless, the sky's the limit...
The journey ahead is what I will delight in...

Each new day brings its own surprises...
The excitement builds, and my heart rises...
With each step I take, my spirit soars...
The world becomes mine and so much more...

My next chapter filled with hope...
Take the leap, learn to cope...
Turn the page, and start anew...
With faith in myself, and in all that I can do...

The story ahead is one written by me...
Joy and love that I long to see...
I will find strength in the storm, hope in the rain...
As it kisses my skin...
With every setback, I will rise again...

The journey may be long, and the road may be
steep...
Hope in my heart is one that runs deep...
There will be more peaks, and there'll be valleys too...
Keep moving forward, with my sights in view...

Next chapter is mine to create...
A story of love, courage, and fate...
Each word, each page of my life...
Spirit will shine, with unyielding light...

So, I'll take that step, and start anew...
As life unfolds and reveals what is true...
Each passing day that goes by...
Next chapter will be a beautiful high...

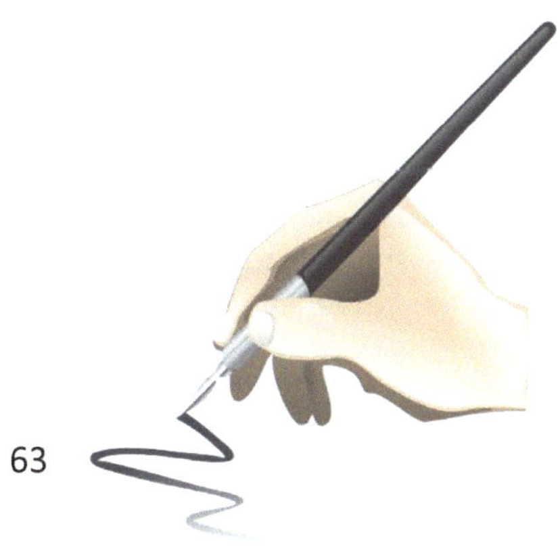

THE AUTHOR

Tha Ono was born and raised on the beautiful island of Trinidad, where he spent most of his childhood surrounded by family and friends. He showed an early interest in education and, after completing his high school education, he decided to pursue a Bachelor of Education in Special Education.

Tha Ono started his teaching career in Trinidad and quickly discovered a natural talent for working with children who have special needs. His passion for teaching and helping students grow soon became his life's mission, and he continued to refine his skills and knowledge in special education by attending workshops, seminars, and teaching courses.

Despite Tha Ono's passion for teaching, he had always loved writing poetry since he was a kid. However, everything changed when his mother died in

2012. After her loss, Tha Ono lost his passion for writing and struggled to find the motivation and inspiration to create. It wasn't until the onset of Covid-19 that Tha Ono's passion for writing was rekindled, and he began self-publishing on Amazon.

Tha Ono's writing quickly gained attention, and he won several poetic prizes over the past few years. He describes his own writing style as one that reflects life experiences - both the good and the bad - and aims to inspire and encourage others to never give up on their dreams.

Tha Ono is an avid animal rights activist and has a deep love for all kinds of animals. He believes that every living being deserves respect and protection, and he tries to give a voice to those who cannot speak for themselves. Tha Ono frequently volunteers at local animal shelters and donates to various animal welfare organizations to support their causes.

Today, Tha Ono continues to teach and write, and he hopes to inspire others to live their best lives, no matter what obstacles they may face. He believes that anyone can achieve their goals with hard work, dedication, and a never-give-up attitude.

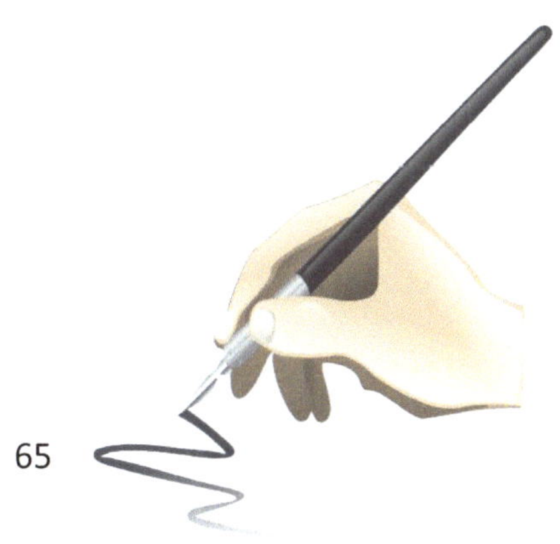